FROM THE FALCON'S NEST

FROM THE
FALCON'S NEST

Bromyard Poetry for Pleasure Group

From the Falcon's Nest
Compiled by Bryony Cullum for the Bromyard Poetry for Pleasure Group

Published by Aspect Design 2015
Malvern, Worcestershire, United Kingdom.

Designed, printed and bound by Aspect Design
89 Newtown Road, Malvern, Worcs. WR14 1PD
United Kingdom
Tel: 01684 561567
E-mail: allan@aspect-design.net
Website: www.aspect-design.net

Cover Design Copyright © 2015 Aspect Design
Original photograph Copyright © Denis R.H. Teal 2015
ISBN 978-1-908832-76-4

CONTENTS

PREFACE

by *Margaret Dallow*..9

TRIBUTE

to Josie Ann Dolan – *Lawrence Randle*...10

MISCELLANEOUS

Gossamer Dreams – *Denis R.H. Teal*...14
An Ancient Race – *Josie Ann Dolan* 14
Adrift – *Val Randle* 16
Poppy – *Sophia Dimmock*..17
Conversation in Knighton – *Peter Holliday*...18
Mother Tongue – *Elizabeth Darcy Jones*...19
Teardrops and Raindrops – *Jane Dallow*...21
Drenched – *VeeBee*...22
Writing a Villanelle – *Barbara M Stewart* 24
100 Years Remembered – *Celia Rees* 25

PLACES

Bromyard – *Dave Hubble*..28
Midnight - Old Portsmouth – *Dorothy Kennedy* 29
Tintern Abbey – *VeeBee*...30
The Hours Bookshop and Café – *Charles Gordon Clark*..............................32
Recollections of the Dart – *Bryony Cullum* 33
Snow on La Plagne – *John Pare*..35
Poetry in Presteign – *Dorothy Kennedy*...36
Nature Walk – *Josie Ann Dolan* 37

LIFE

Now You Are One – *Maggie McGladdery* 40
Isabel Aged 3 – *Lawrence Randle* 41
Needs No Proving – *Elizabeth Darcy Jones* 42
Moving House – *Judy Malet* 42
Who Am I? – *Thalia Gordon Clark* 43
Her Sea of Dreams – *Maggie McGladdery* 44
On the Train – *Val Randle* 46
Ups and Downs – *Dave Hubble* 47
Ten Generations Back – *Charles Gordon Clark* 48
Room at the Top of the Stairs – *Maggie McGladdery* 49
Peace and Tranquillity – *Shirley Whittall* 50
Mind Games – *Tiercel of the March* 51
The Guitar Player – *Sophia Dimmock* 52
Farmer's Boy – *Peter Holliday* 53
Alzheimers – Respite A Carer's Response – *Judy Malet* 54
Awaken – *Sophia Dimmock* 54
The Davies Sisters Collection – *Charles Gordon Clark* 55
True Friendship – *Tiercel of the March* 56

THE SEASONS

A September Walk – *Margaret Dallow* 60
Border Hymns – *Peter Holliday* 61
Spring – *Barbara M Stewart* 62
Three Quarters – *VeeBee* 62
Golden Memories – *Margaret Dallow* 63
Inspiration or Cold Comfort – *Lawrence Randle* 64

WAR / DEATH

Figures on the Foreshore – *Peter D Hollingsworth* 68
And the Poppies will Forever be Red – *Denis R.H. Teal* 69
Certainty – *John Pare* 70

The Deepest Silence – *Celia Rees* 73
Abandonment – *Peter D Hollingsworth* 73
Women at War – *Celia Rees* 76
The Gunner's Horse – *Barbara M Stewart* 77

HUMOUR

The Cabbage – *Margaret Dallow* 80
Praise Poem to the Worm – *Gill Fothergill* 81
Fool's Gold – *Denis R.H. Teal* 82
Just a Potato – *Judy Malet* 83
Salad Sonata – *Shirley Whittall* 84
Meghalaya Cloud Tea – *Elizabeth Darcy Jones* 85
I am an Amoeba – *Dave Hubble* 86
On Hearing Something on Radio 4 About Plastic Daffodils –
    Thalia Gordon Clark 88

THE NATURAL WORLD

Seaspell – *Lawrence Randle* 90
Creation – *John Pare* 91
Was It? – *Bryony Cullum* 92
Song of the Earth – *Jane Dallow* 95
After Felling – *Thalia Gordon Clark* 96
The Valley Through the Window – *Josie Ann Dolan* 97
The Miracle of the Garden – *Dorothy Kennedy* 98
Whistle Down the Wind – *Jane Dallow* 98
A Colourful Day – *Bryony Cullum* 100
Rosemarie's Vision – *Rosemarie Powell* 101
The Peregrine Falcon – *Tiercel of the March* 102

AND FINALLY...

The Long and Short of It – *Dave Hubble* 105

ILLUSTRATIONS/ART WORK by

Vee Bee
Bryony Cullum
Jane Dallow
Margaret Dallow
Maggie McGladdery
Val Randle

Bromyard Poetry Group Members would like to thank
Sylvia at The Falcon Hotel, Bromyard
for providing them with a nest,
more properly an eyrie.

PREFACE

On returning with my friend, Ann Dolan, from a poetry meeting in Hereford, we decided that this was something we could do together. With her knowledge of poetry and my organisational skills, we could form a poetry group for Bromyard. This we did, resulting in meetings with other poets, exploring the work of well known writers and having a venue to air our own poems. Poetry for Pleasure offers an opportunity to share and enjoy many types of verse.

Sadly, Ann is no longer with us but her spirit lives on in her wonderful poetry and is still an inspiration to our group which is now in its twelfth year. During this time, we have grown in number and have listened to a wide variety of poetry written by our members.

We thought we would capture some and produce a book and we hope that others will enjoy reading it.

Margaret Dallow
Co-founder and Chair of Bromyard Poetry for Pleasure

The group now meets monthly in The Falcon Hotel, Bromyard in Falcon Mews (the old theatre projection room). Hence we thought a fitting title for the book would be *From the Falcon's Nest*.

JOSIE ANN DOLAN

(1943 – 2008)

Tomorrow they put the tree up in the square
And the lights on in the High Street.
Today one of the lights went out.
For she will not be there.

Her light illuminated a primrosed ruin of a church
Holding precious memories for many a child.
It shone on the glory days of golden hops
In Bromyard, and the elegance of royal gloves.
It lit up the hedgerows, the shady woods
And many a sacred grove.

And she was very Bromyard.
Part of the spirit of the place;
Matter of fact, self-deprecating,
Persevering, curious, interesting.
God knows her life was hard.
She was inventive, making light of setbacks
And of illness. She had to be creative.
She got on with life,
Valuing tradition, yet not afraid to change it,
Skilled at improvisation
Which people here call getting on and making do.

There is a stream of talent in this place
Which comes from deep within the earth:-
Music, dancing, stories, poems, drama,
Puddings of delight, and costumes of all ages.
And she was part of that,
And we will carry on
Come rain, hell, high water
Or disparagement.
And in so doing, we will honour her.
And we shall not forget.

Lawrence Randle

Lawrence Randle was an original member of the group.
His tribute to Ann was written on behalf of us all.

MISCELLANEOUS

GOSSAMER DREAMS

If thoughts were butterflies
And wind chimes were words
If clouds were a carpet
And stars wild birds

If hilltops were the seabed
And eagles were whales
And the webs of small spiders
Were billowing sails,

If the milky way was a river
That flowed to the sea
And the wind was a prison
That had no key.

If dewdrops were silver
And sunsets were gold
We would all have a fortune
Too large to hold.

Denis R H Teal

AN ANCIENT RACE

Blue smoke curls, through the canopy of oaks,
Wood burning scents the air.
Sunshine warms the morning chill,
The grass is wet still with dew.

I wait beside the hawthorn hedge,
watching the gypsy woman tend the fire,
stooping she stirs the porridge in the pot.
Grey hair she braids around her head,
Today she wears a skirt of scarlet plaid,
Covered with an apron white as snow.

In a little while she turns
Her brown lined face to me,
Calls me with her hand.
Smiles a toothless smile, dark eyes meet mine,
Over the gate I quickly climb.

A caravan painted yellow and red stands near,
Between its shafts sits the gypsy man.
At his feet shavings scatter from pegs he's made,
Strips of tin bind each one,
He fills the willow basket up.

He pours mugs of tea from the brown teapot,
Bids me sit to share a breakfast feast.
Tethered close, their piebald horse
Quietly crops the summer grass.
Romany these two, a proud and ancient race,
This their final journey made
to rest old wearied bones they say,
we spoon the porridge from fine china bowls,
and only the wind whispers by.

Josie Ann Dolan

The gypsies were an annual and integral part of the rural scene in counties
like Herefordshire, relied upon to undertake many agricultural tasks like hop
picking. The same families would reappear year by year and Ann had fond
memories of the group who came to Avenbury and were very kind to her.

ADRIFT

Look children at the fish
the blue-nosed one with deckchair stripes
the orange shy one and silver smartsuit
oh so refined,
and the bugle bead tetra
streaming turquoise jewels.

And look the rocks are jade
and violet and burnt umber
and silken marble white.
see the ones with old bouquets
of rusty roses, stiffened fern
and eggshell petals,

We used to live in the sea once
before we moved to land
and our bodies weighted
to heaviness and sinews tightened,
and our skin lost the rainbows,
only our eyes still shone
as the water mirrors.

We can still float and glide
in the water but our cities
are on land where
traffic flows instead.

One day bring me here
and leave me in the ocean.
let me drift with the weeds
and crumble with sand.
I'll shine then
under the moon.

Val Randle

POPPY

My muddy finger prints on the blood red poppy.
I knew it would be beautiful and I wanted it to be mine.
With garden hands I prised its petals open, like a forced kiss,
To look inside and see its love before it was ready to be on show.
Its centre glared black so I let it go. Tightly it closed.
Like other things in life I try to own,
I stamped the poppy, marked it with a code.
My muddy finger prints on the blood red poppy, now open
And it still isn't mine.

Sophia Dimmock

Poppy is a personal confession. The poem stems from a true experience of
mine as a young girl impatient to see a poppy bloom in the garden. The poem
extends to become an honest reflection of my human failings.

CONVERSATION IN KNIGHTON

"Have you ever been to London?"
"No. I've been to Brecon. Once.
Before the war. By charabanc.
An open top job. We got back late –
Lost in the mountains. There was such a frost
The trees were cracking! You could hear them
Snap as we drove past! The last few miles
We fairly slid downhill – out of gear –
To save petrol. Old Cyril Price
Had bought an extra can just in case.
As we came up from Knucklas
I heard town clock strike three. My cap
Was frozen to my head. My hands were blue!
The wife was worried sick. The dogs
Distraught, yelping and whimpering –
After that I resolved to travel
No further than my legs would carry me –
Or a good horse! What should I do in London?"

How could I answer? His eyes like the sky?
His skin an autumn fruit warmed by the sun.
I recalled the faces of my city friends:
Anxious, nervous, pale as smoke;
Their movements hurried; their statements sharp.
I shook my head slowly, and he smiled.
"Good day to you!" he said, and strolled away.

Peter Holliday

MOTHER TONGUE

Matru, when you birthed the earth's first Mother tongue
What instinct put the silent hum of being in your name?
Motina
Maji
Mutter
Moeder
Mum
The sound is just the same in almost every language:
Chapped old or young lopsided lips suckle on a breath of warm
And what comes next is too familiar to express
Represents a constant that we're bound by forces far too strong
Ever to remember
And yet
She's all that we come from

Matru, Mother of the space in which the 'a' and 'ah' exist
Did you plant them in a kiss in
Amma
Anya
Haha
Nana
And in Abatyse?
We can't escape the marriage to your child-man –
But with your ears attuned to Love we listen
Hear the sound that ties, unites us with
An unseen uncut cord made of something other
Gentle presence
Mantra of the masses
Mother.

Elizabeth Darcy Jones

TEARDROPS AND RAINDROPS

Rain, my face wet,
teardrops mixed with rain drops
running together down my face,
touching my lips, tasting
salty from my tears.

The trees in the park
are bowed, drooping
their branches, reaching towards me
like arms to embrace me…comfort me,
their sighing is like my crying.

As I walk on,
raindrops fall from the trees.
I lift my face to their coolness
until the salt from my tears
washes away and only
the trees know I'm crying.

Jane Dallow

DRENCHED

Turn me on
I'll pour myself all over you.
Dreamy-eyed beneath me you are
barely awake.
I will find every crevice
every precious fold of you.
Do you want me hot?

Maybe a little cooler
or somewhere in between.
I will come on to you strong
if you want it
or I can be less forceful
but your hand
is in control.
Let my searching silky fingers
trickle through your tumbled curls.
Throw back your head
I will multi-kiss your throat
and leave a sparkle
on your lips
and a tingle
at the very tip of your tongue.
Shrug your glistening shoulders –
seamlessly they swerve, slant
into the smooth arch of your back.
Let my sateen spray caress
your ripe unblushing breast,
and tease your tiny trinket toes
pretty as pink pearls
shimmering in the splash
of dancing rainbows.

Soak up every jewelled drop of me
then stop me dead
before I overflow.

VeeBee

WRITING A VILLANELLE

My mind's a blank, the words they will not come,
My pencil hovers, staggers and retreats,
To prime the pan and flash the rhyming gun.

I idle hours away through days of sun,
Spring, summer, autumn, winter, all complete,
My mind's a blank, the words they will not come.

I scan the daily papers of the Sun,
The Times, Observer, all so full of meat,
To prime the pan and flash the rhyming gun.

I thumb the library's every heavy tome
Stretching my mind for every metre's feet.
My mind's a blank, the words they will not come.

I shred the later hours, all ideas blown,
rewriting every line as obsolete,
to prime the pan and flash the rhyming gun.

To write a villanelle cannot be done,
Without Thesaurus lying at my feet,
My mind's a blank, the words they will not come
To prime the pan and flash the rhyming gun.

Barbara M Stewart

100 YEARS REMEMBERED

A world war gobbled many nations' young,
Males marched away and females worked unsung,
Love of country, a will to do one's share,
Stood bravely in the mud and blood out there.

Women and girls stepped out to work the land,
Munitions made with nimble fingered hands,
Kept home fires burning, families afloat,
And in those years attained the right to vote.

Ideas blossomed, changes followed fast,
The motor bikes and cars left folk aghast,
And then the wonder of the aeroplane,
How did it stay up there – please do explain.

Letters with crossed lines or scripted well,
Gave way to that contraption made by Bell,
The telephone. But one could sit and chat
Till handsets and then mobiles stopped all that.

Slate, chalk, paper and pen, told their story
In crafted sentences, and words of glory.
Emails came in shorter and much quicker.
Txtd sentences were even slickr.

Hems rose to show an ankle, what a thrill,
Then higher went and higher, higher still!
Trousers flared and shirts gave way to tees
Fashions flourished above and below the knees.

Life moves fast, faster and the world grows small,
People live longer, buildings spread, grow tall,
Green spaces vanish, nature under threat
Knowledge has grown, still grows, not finished yet.

But some things haven't changed and never will,
The young are critical of elders still,
Things aren't as good as they were used to be
In days when we were young and so carefree.

Celia Rees

PLACES

BROMYARD

I fell in love with Bromyard, way back in '88,
last Century, of course, that was; in case you doubt the date!
It's such a friendly place to know, find shopping there is great,
and even total strangers are wont to call me mate;

I'm from 'The Smoke' origin'ly, that's London don't you know,
but 'Adolf' sent me down the road to Cornwall; there to grow.
Then back to 'town' & then to Kent, (from whence the soil doth blow),
'n' Sussex next, where, (just like Kent), the pace is fast, not slow.

Those counties, mostly crowded, are busy, loud, 'n' full,
and seldom do you see there, the wondrous Her'ford bull.
So often too, they're full right up, until the winter's lull,
but in the summer weather, just see the crowds they pull.

Bromyard is full of strangers, that I've known all my life,
they often stop and chat with me, or me trouble and me strife.
And though we live in Pencombe, where seldom trouble's rife,
if we ever move at all's Bromyard for me and Wife.

You get a bright "Good morning", even when it ain't,
and frequently some smile at me, (is this because I'm quaint?).
Th' whole county's very nice as well, with views to make you faint,
and rovers oft return of course; we've now too; otter's spraint.

And so you see, I'm townie-born, but I was country-bred,
and therefore hope, only t' leave this place, when I am dead!
I still might stay, depending where, they fin'lly lay my head,
but if I do, I ask you please; do not my spirit dread.

Dave Hubble

MIDNIGHT – OLD PORTSMOUTH

The water laps with quiet splash against the harbour walls
The rigging rattles eerily, a lonely seagull calls.
A thousand orange lights reflect on water dark and deep,
The towns around the harbour are quietly asleep.
The whisper of ghosts from ages past flitter silently by,
The masts of the Warrior and Victory still reach towards the sky.
The sailors of the Mary Rose laugh and gamble, unaware
Of disaster and a watery grave awaiting them out there.
Cheering crowds line harbour walls for Britannia's farewell visit,
The sending off and welcome home of warship, sub and frigate.
Tonight the old ghosts fall asleep as shadows sift and sigh
While out upon the water, a ferry slides swiftly by.

Dorothy Kennedy

My sister lives in Southsea. I find the Old Portsmouth and the historic
dockyard very atmospheric. If only those harbour walls could talk what
stories they could tell!

TINTERN ABBEY

Reaching, searching, pointing to the heavens.
Brushing eternity with gentle, fragile fingers.

Washed in radiant eventide, a single sigh whispers
through the cloisters. Mournful, disturbed.
You hide your face in your own dark shadow,
listening for the deeper silence
locked away for ever with soft footfalls of the past.
Your discomposure was born when
Merry Henry at a stroke closed your doors
and raised the roof. Stripped of lead your
rafters crumbled, ceilings perished, slipped
in dust to the ground. Death,
decay and desolation…
                    Dissolute.

Fading daylight dances on your altar
through gaping skylights now lending shelter to
clattering, restless rooks, freewheeling
on the winds of change.
None shall ever share your close-held secrets.
No memory of wrongful word or act have you disclosed
to any on this earth.
Time's atrocities have neither trespassed nor
dared to search within your unknown depths.
And will not…
                    Resolute.

Enigmatic. Inestimable. Immovable.
Ravaged by storms of damaging acid rain,
sharp and angry rocks of hail, hammered by the
winter gales, forcibly entering yet failing
impotently to penetrate the guardian of your soul.
The daily gallery of prying eyes, visiting
from established, educated, sheltered worlds
chatter, nod and smile into their guidebooks,
then, satisfied, tick you off... move on,
telephotos scanning other sights on the itinerary.

Nine centuries have failed to dim your presence,
your glory or your magnitude.
Awesome, ageless and enduring...
                    Absolute.

                    VeeBee

THE HOURS BOOKSHOP AND CAFE, BRECON

Coming back to a town you know well –
Like putting on a comfortable suit
You've more or less grown out of; but still
A feeling of being back home – "home's where
When you turn up, they have to take you in" –
So said the poet wisely decades ago –
And we're welcomed in – paying of course
For our lunch and our books, but here
She remembers our names, who we are – two years
Not too long to be still, somehow, at home –

So many homes scattered across the land –
Not all I can still put on with the same
Comfort – but not entirely grown out of either –
And now – how long before all the homes are worn out?
How long until totally different clothes
Are appropriate? Or naked, homeless,
Anima vagula, blandula – is it right
To wander in anticipation past those rails
Of empty hangers, through those lifeless towns –

When soup's on the table, juice in the glass,
Immediate prospect of glorious sounds –
Tosca in Cardiff – feigned deaths – drive home in the dark –
To wait – wait for the last fitting – the last
Viewing of what will be the very last home.

Charles Gordon Clark

Written in this cafe on National Poetry Day 2013
when invited to "Write us a poem!"

RECOLLECTIONS OF THE DART

I start my appreciation of the Dart
Amongst damp niches in the peat
Sustaining sphagnum, sedge, sundew, bog cotton and rush,
Gradually grouping, filtering, seeping
Seeking the downhill path.

It's in the open, in a miniature valley,
Then trickling shallowly over gravel.
It becomes a rivulet, bouncing, chuckling, pouring, sliding,
Brushing boulders, bracken, whortleberries, heather, gorse and grasses.

Wider now, sometimes deeper, rill and pool and waterfall.
Water creatures, stickleback and minnow, damselflies, dragonflies,
Caddis flies and others. Never far away on land great big, black slugs.
Its environment provides a whole miscellany of life.

Ponies, cattle, sheep come to drink.
Too wide for stride or jump,
It bubbles and swishes or silently passes
Gradually enlarging, attracting such as heron, curlew, dipper,
Wagtail; eyed by buzzard, skylark and pipit.

Those boulders, lichen or moss covered,
Massive, hefty, solid stones
Bedazzled with quartz, mica and feldspar,
Often water smoothed, flattened for a firm footfall.

Routeways have to cross with ford, stepping stones or bridges,
Historical tracks and clappers,
Roads and native granite stalwarts, straddle the water,
Often with three arches aloof from the flow,
Postbridge, Belliver, Huccaby, Holne,
Yet sometimes overflowed.

Some notable woods line its banks.
Wistman's Wood, ancient, with weird, twisted oak;
The gorge steeply covered by timber
Shields the river whether in calm or spate.

Growing older now, the Dart flows serenely
Past Buckfast Abbey and limestone caves at Buckfastleigh. Onwards
Flanked by road and rail, through luscious countryside to
Dartington, and historic Totnes, port and head of tidal flow.

Leaving the site of business, industry, quayside and boats.
The river now of major size
Exhibits a ria, deep depths product of a rise in sea levels,
Shelter for Her Majesty's fleet,
And myriads of marina pleasure craft
As well as livings made from fish and boats.

Dart, a jewel of natural habitats,
Vistas of bare moorland, agriculture and forest,
Provides so much for man's needs, water supplies from leat to reservoirs.
For farms, industry, pleasure, leisure, to observe with wonder.

The peaty colouration of icy, clear water,
A joy to dip a toe, dabble a hand, submerge
In its lovely, lively softness and wild water swim.
A home for salmon, species of trout and lesser known fish,
But, beware of ferocious hollows, sudden gushes,
Tidal surges or major floods.

Three ferries link the townships of Kingswear and Dartmouth,
The top ferry, a historical feature as it is cable bound.
Downstream the Dart washes past a castle on either bank,
With a final kink it reaches the open sea,
An insert into the beautiful Devonshire coastline,
The magnificent River Dart.

Bryony Cullum

August 2014

SNOW ON LA PLAGNE

The mountain turrets soar and pierce the sky,
But cloud and scudding snow deceive the eye,
Now veiling, now revealing scattered trees:
Now showing steep and risk-fraught rocky screes.
Amidst this landscape frosty and severe
Move figures,
Sometimes sharp, but oft less clear,
Who glide like ghosts across the wintry alps
With hoods and helmets cosseting their scalps.
The snow still swirls about the eerie town,

Now seen as if through tulle, or goose's down,
While tiny humans trudge through snow-filled streets
To fetch back food, or infant-favoured treats,
To temporary homes where they can rest
And dream of clear runs out along the crest.

John Pare

POETRY IN PRESTEIGN

Sunday. A quiet November afternoon.
Gazing through elegant arched windows
At painted flowers opposite, I am transported far away;
Freewheeling down sand dunes, bleached marram grass,
Thunder clouds looming, stumbling across love letters-
Blue ribbon, fine paper, copperplate handwriting.
Gazing at kaleidoscope colours
Reflected from shards of broken glass.
I hear Brian Boru's army marching nearer,
Bodhrans banging, pipes playing, fog swirling…fading away.
Seventeenth century Spanish dancers.
Dark, haughty, stamping feet.
My reverie is broken – tea!
Plates of cakes on the grand piano, round blue tea pot,
Fine china Coronation mugs.
Outside, darkness has claimed the painted flowers.
Beautiful language flows again.
New images are conjured.
Fairy tale frozen landscape,

Cracked ice on a frozen river,
A swan that has lost its mate.
Soup bubbling, bread baking,
The poet's red haired mother, aspirational, wearing stiletto heels.
We leave, enriched and privileged,
Into the quiet Radnorshire night.

Dorothy Kennedy

2014

I wrote this after going to a poetry reading by Gillian Clarke in the Assembly Rooms at Presteign. Gillian Clarke was delayed and we were entertained by a classical guitarist and a local poetry group, who read aloud a selection of their poems. I hoped to capture some of the magic of the poetry whereby a short text can conjure up such vivid pictures and emotions.

NATURE WALK

Earthy odours drift in the humid air.
We tramp the woodlands muddied path,
Where slender campions grow, amongst the ladies lace,
Sharing space with stinging nettle clumps,
Trailing down between slim sleek trees,
From shadows into sunshine we emerge.
We stand bemused to see,
Two wire men striding out on stilts,
Weathered blackened, an artist's tribute to another time,
Telling how the hops of Herefordshire,
On poles and wires were strung.

Beyond, framed by two great oaks
A lake lies shimmering.
Bright yellow flags, bulrushes in beige browns drape the edge,
And pale purple rhododendrons,
On black green bushes bloom.

Liver spotted spaniels swim, for some thrown stick,
And on the wooden bench a man and woman sit,
I recognise him, though his hair is snowy white,
His face is deeply lined.
I feel unease with time,
So far behind our schooldays seem.

We pass with pleasantries, "Hello, how are you?"
To group before the yellow flags,
We pose for a family photograph.
I turn to see the dogs, and they are gone,
Down some other woodland path.

Josie Ann Dolan

This is a poem written by Ann who had so many associations with
Brockhampton and whose family did much work and forestry on the estate.
It was a very special place for her and where she went to school.

LIFE

NOW YOU ARE ONE

As this is your first, I thought I'd explain,
About birthdays and parties and all they contain.
You wake up excited, so no difference there,
Mum will dress you up smartly and arrange your hair.
Dad will blow up balloons and make sure the food's right
And so that it's special, he'll have stayed up all night.
Your friends will arrive, with boxes and smiles
Some from next door and some travelled miles.
There'll be paper and ribbons to fight your way through
To presents that people have brought just for you.
Your brother will giggle and join in the fun
They'll all sing 'Happy Birthday' to Ollie, who's one!!!

We're sad we can't be there to see all your fun,
But we wish all that's good for our smallest grandson.

Maggie McGladdery

(Grandma)

ISABEL AGED 3

Did you know ballet was a martial art?
Isabel does, she's very smart.
Should anyone threaten or try to outdo her
She wiggles her tutu
Saying, "Anything you can do
I can do too."

Isabel's hair is out of control
Curly and blonde
It's really wild.
Of her hair she's very fond.
Should anyone of her hair lay hold
Isabel will get you.
Isabel is really wild.
Isabel is A WILD CHILD.

And how does ice cream
Make her feel.
When cold and creamy
It slips down her throat
Does she feel anything of note?
"Happy," says Isabel.

Lawrence Randle

NEEDS NO PROVING

I think mothering's an ancient type of bread
Strong robust umami rich
Its flour love-seeded with humour
Soft and nourishing as spelt
Its yeast pungent fresh with all things felt and live
Born absorbing yielding always just enough to rise
Moistened with tears and other liquids
(don't ask what, but none denied)
Unquestioned staple
Especially in times of war
Goes well with crowds, fishes
And innumerable other dishes
Takes endless kneading
Generates its own heat
Only designated one day's rest.

Elizabeth Darcy Jones

MOVING HOUSE

So we're here,
The months of looking and momentary living in every
strange house we saw, are over.
Our things are out and around us.
Bare floors – bleak windows.
I look up and unloved trees and unknown light leap
at me.

We are here, but my mind is still with familiar walls –
Benches shaping window views known through all and
many seasons.
Views so etched – they will not go away
Rooms of memories.
First cots
Someone old forever in a certain corner bed.
Door noises opening – shutting.
I look up at strange windows…
My woman's heart cries.

Judy Malet

WHO AM I?

First of course
There was a form to fill in.
There had to be a name
A place of birth,
An address – if not "as above".

Then under the form, endless paper,
The questions, the daily stuff,
What am I thinking?
What am I feeling?
Each one has its coming
And its going.
None have a permanence,
Like litter blown about
All colours, bright, dark, pale, dull.

Gathering them in my hands,
I discover beneath
The light which gives the colour,
The whole spectrum of light.
My fingers, dipping,
Become rainbow tinted
Just for a moment.
In delight I play
Up to my elbows
My toes dance in and out.
Then it's lost – littered with more stuff.

Another day, another moment,
A glimpse of rainbow.

Thalia Gordon Clark

HER SEA OF DREAMS

She lies on her sea of dreams
Not drowning, but waving
At a world full of viewers.
Viewers on their own voyages,
Gender and experience influencing their perspective
And destination.
She, content – embodiment of woman
Relaxed and laying bare the soul;
With liberation of mind, body, spirit.

None of the past anxiety
That fed on insecurities,
Obtained through women's collective saga.

Continuing her journey
To where no surgeon's knife is needed,
No embarrassment felt,
No discomfort, no angst.
Comfortable with who she is,
– who we are,
– who I am.

Maggie McGladdery

ON THE TRAIN

Two men guarding space
laptops carefully placed
shut out hopeful entrants.
one man bullying the guard
for his failed reservation and
she takes out her frustration
on a mild baggaged student.
and a whistle blows.
ugly sidings, storage and
building debris give way to
shreds of sky, some trees and
houses by the track with
garden stage sets we watch
in hope of players.
the phones start up.
over hearings of other lives
where mothers are dying and
sons tell sisters of their crying.
where someone excuses her
demands before a funeral.
where meetings in pubs are
arranged and thank yous
for last night.
and another station under
cold grey sky draws up outside
there's struggling and swinging
bags and banging doors and
flopping down all round.
and a whistle blows.

there's texting and games and
pages flick as scenes flicker.
Little rivers and bridges into
mystery groves and a hare loping.
no stage but my longed for
haven to plunge into
run through the dusk fields
escaping all in a child's hoping.
now six graceful schoolgirls are
seat swapping, doubling up
smiling and twittering
making the space huge and
we crumpled people
non – existent.
another stop.
a shuffling exodus bottlenecks
on the platform to climb steps.
Silent now three girls scatter
To each car to stow bags
Under parental smiles
and we are left behind.
wistful for our own greeting
Still distant up the line
and a whistle blows.

Val Randle

UPS AND DOWNS

I must go up to the Downs again, and then to Bromyard Town,
and on to Bringsty Common and Warren's leafy crown.

To stroll among the bracken, and breathe the clean, clean, air,
And listen to a skylark and try to see him there.

And, as I slowly stroll, alone or not, and ramble,
Past buttercup, the damson trees, and dodge the searching bramble.

I see ascending flocks of chaffinches and plovers,
And watch my feet, lest I disturb; a pair of clover lovers!

And when I feel the need to wander down the road,
imbibe a drink or have a snack, see people, as they strode.

Yes, down into that sleepy town, [it's only people bustle!],
And everywhere, folk stop to chat, and form a knot or hustle.

I only need a loaf of bread, could take me half an hour,
I'm bound to see some folk I know, it's part of country's bower.

I'm also sure to see some folks I know just by sight,
Or have forgot the name of; embarrassing, but slight!

We often pop to Bromyard, from Pencombe, light or dark,
Just to be there; not because, we need a place to park!

Bromyard brings out best from folk, the people and those smiles,
To walk enough to miss one, you'd have to walk for miles.

It takes much fewer muscles to smile instead of frown,
So, once again it's leisurely to wander through our town.

And as for smiles, they're worthless, that's what people say,
Smiles are worth nothing at all; 'til given all away.

Dave Hubble

TEN GENERATIONS BACK, EVERYONE HAS 1000 ANCESTORS
(1024, to be precise)

A thousand couplings – passionate or calm?
The pregnancies desired? Unplanned? Resented?
A thousand nine months' carryings –
A thousand births –
And all the babies lived!
We're talking Stuart times maybe –
The chance a child lived? 50-50? Less?
Yet, these all survived, grew up, and found
A mate among the thousand.

The couplings recommenced – again the babies lived,
500 now – negotiated all
The hazards, ills and shocks,
To mate themselves among that cohort,
All those chance occurrences
That needed happen,
All the random acts of fate
That just these pairings sorted out,
Producing in their progeny that one from each
Who'd mate within the dwindling band,
And then again – and now at 64
The date is 17 – what? – 80? – 95?
And still the shaking dice bring those
In couples, and their children too.

It's now 16 – and that's your granddad's granddad,
Grandma's grandma – Queen Victoria's on the throne
And now the chances babies live are getting good,
But still there're all those hazards to endure
Until they're fertile, can set up a home.

Well, they got through, their kids who meet, do too,
It's getting much more likely you'll be you!
And then your parents meet and mate –
Pure chance, it wasn't really fate –
It's you at last – how much you owe
To all those couplings long ago!

Charles Gordon Clark

ROOM AT THE TOP OF THE STAIRS
(On returning to Art after 40 years in the wilderness)

I came to find colour
Its depths and mysteries

I came – so I thought – to discover
How to present the surface of the world
The vision of depth through shades of pigment

I came to discover what was lost over time
That part of me I had (freely) given away
Energy sapped over years.

I came to find help on my journey
To unlock the trapped, the repressed.
Thick slashes of paint so eager to display
The pent up years of expression.

I came to find colour
...and I discovered – myself.

Maggie McGladdery

PEACE AND TRANQUILLITY

What is peace and tranquillity?
To me it is getting away from reality
To ease your mind into a world of dreams
Where fairies dance on the bubbles in streams
When shadows from the fire creep up the wall
The sound of the clock chiming in the hall
The whisper of the wind as it tickles in the leaves
The flutter of birds nesting in the eaves
The mist as it floats in the valley below
A rainbow that curves around in a bow
Listening to music that moves the soul
Relaxed and calm you have reached your goal
Free of tension and worry as you enjoy the flow
Peace and tranquillity is now yours to own.

Shirley Whittall

MIND GAMES

A faraway look in those old faraway eyes
Of a faraway place beneath faraway skies
A memory, fleeting, of a chuckling stream
An old grassy bank and a forgotten dream

An old grey stone school with a resonant bell
Surrounded by Pine trees casting their spell
A best friend to sit by with secrets to share
The unbroken promise and occasional dare

A mindful of memories of times long ago
Springtime and summer, autumn and snow
Sung Christmas carols so sweet on the ear
Snowdrops, Primroses blooming each year

Memories of a lifetime, so clear and so bright
First love's faces on the pillow each night
Hopes for the future or regrets for the past
Losing those loved ones around us at last

All those poignant memories of a life led
Words said to hurt, should never be said
Far too late now for the words to retract
No one left to hear them and that is a fact

But what of a journey that may lie ahead
As a mind cannot die, so it has been said
Perhaps to awake on a far distant shore
The old world is lost to the mind evermore

As warm waves lap at pure golden sand
And loved ones waiting, all close at hand
With all cares and worries left far behind
What peace and joy are forever entwined

Maybe that is the reasoning called déjà vu
Far away feelings that keep coming through
Your mind saying you've been here before
And one day for sure you will open that door

John Elmes   Tiercel of the March

THE GUITAR PLAYER

He played his soul for us to hear.
It rocked between the characters of others,
Telling of our stories, reverberating fears.
Then there was something more,
Beyond eternal unity, an amalgamation of man
And rhapsody of dawn.
It spoke of him, his form could not reveal.
It feels like ten men strumming every chord.
I want to listen,
Take it with me,
Stain my essence.
I want it closer to me, running through me,
Not to slip away when he is done and
We applaud.

Sophia Dimmock

The Guitar Player is a poem which appreciates the way music speaks to
people; how it reaches people at a different level. I wrote the poem as I
was compelled to put the notion into words.

FARMER'S BOY

I might be docking mangolds
In a long field smudged by rain
On the edge of nowhere,

Humming an old song to myself –
Or whistling – whistling
Like a blackbird in the hedge.

Or I'm clearing out pigs
And tapping on a hurdle
The riddle of a fiddle

I'd heard the night before
In the 'Bottle and Glass' –
That's the sort of man I am!

But remember, I can't write,
Read, draw, compose a sentence,
Count more than my fingers will let me –

So I wander out with a mug in my fist,
Lie on my back in the mucky yard,

And watch the cloud-shapes
Shift across the blue.

Peter Holliday

ALZHEIMER'S – RESPITE
A Carer's Response.

I come in the door, and it is
As though the house has grown
Since we sadly left together.
An expansion, an empty space –
All because you are no longer here.

I have left you in a ward,
A kindly ward
But I know that even with
The wanderings of your mind,
This is where you would want to be –
At home.

Judy Malet

AWAKEN

It felt like the Earth was new.
Like I dreamt a realisation and
Woke up to the smell of it.
Like I'd just stepped off a plane
To a different place.
Like I'd been born again.
I want to wait in this moment,
Stand in its rain, splash my face.

But I know it won't be long
Until it begins to feel familiar
And then I'll move, and the shine
Becomes the grey.

Sophia Dimmock

THE DAVIES SISTERS' COLLECTION
NATIONAL MUSEUM OF WALES, CARDIFF

Two sisters, rich (inherited not earned
Their money, from the miracle that Wales
Became from iron, coal, rail, the docks. Granddad
Prime mover, beneficiary, a giant) –
These sisters – educated, cultured, shy,
Not made for marriage, motherhood, but fount
Of living – yes, life-giving streams of light,
Of colour, form, of vision, so that Welsh
Lives later are enriched through all that cash.

How so? They bought – on sound advice – from France,
And showered on Wales French light, French vision, French
Impressions of a way to see the world.
Rich gifts we take for granted – but Cezanne,
Pissarro, Monet, Sisley, now are ours.
And we the children of that childless pair
Made pregnant by the artists over there.

Charles Gordon Clark

TRUE FRIENDSHIP

When you are sitting in your garden
There in the twilight of your years
Looking back into your memories
With all their many hopes and fears

Counting up the many blessings
That on you have been bestowed
Fond remembrances of a lifetime
That through your mind echoed

Memories of true friends you've had
Were they like those grains of sand
Or maybe you could only count them
Upon the fingers of one hand

Reaching five? You are so lucky
And if they honestly were true
Not just in fairest weather, but –
Through storms of life with you

But before you smile contentedly
Did you reciprocate as well?
When they too were at their lowest
In their own personal living hell

If so my friend you have been entered
Upon that, most honourable scroll
For giving that true friendship freely
With both an open heart and soul

Then when your journey's finally over
When your eyelids close in sleep
There'll be someone watching over you
From those friendships that you keep.

John Elmes   Tiercel of the March

THE SEASONS

A SEPTEMBER WALK

On a warm September evening
As the daylight recedes
The mist in the valley envelopes the trees.

The velvet air caresses my cheek.
The birds have gone to sleep.
I stop and listen, refresh my soul.

I can hear the pounding hooves
Of a bygone age here
On that old racecourse.

Shouts of the golfers on the green
That the little girl swept for six pence
Before each school day.

How fortunate am I to live in such a place
With views of the Clee, Hay Bluff
And May Hill, down there in far off Gloucestershire

Margaret Dallow

One of the pleasures of living in this corner of Herefordshire, in an old
market town, Bromyard, that nestles beneath the Downs, is being able to
walk out in the countryside.

BORDER HYMNS

Summer's late evening – say eight-thirty, nine –
Thrush still singing from the meadows edge,
Where fields fall steep through alder, ash and oak
To the perpetual river.

Door of the farmhouse open to the air
So swallow and martin dance in and out,
Suspicious cats, dog-tired dogs,
And the last glimmers of daylight.

At the upright polished piano sits
Emmanuel Price of Cae Newydd,
Black boots heavy on the bright brass pedals,
Cap flat on one end of the keyboard
As he sways and chants the bleak old Baptist hymn:

"I need thee every hour."

He tips back the white moon of his head,
Closes his pale blue eyes and lets the words fly free
Around the room, rise to the beams, flow out
Across the threshold, through the green gate
Into each byre and stall, each hutch and pen:

"I need Thee – O, I need Thee –
Every hour I need Thee –
Come quickly and abide
Or life is vain –"

Summer's late evening:
The old man's voice beseeching:
Stars rising over Twyn-y-Garth:
Thrush still singing.

Peter Holliday

61

SPRING

Blackbird nests in my hedge
A ramble of clematis stems,
Keep her hidden
Her tail fanned high
The only indication she is there.

The Japanese cherry in full bloom
Long branches stretch in graceful curves,
Dominates my garden, a cold March wind
Tosses tiny blossoms,
Fills the air like snow.

Barbara M Stewart

THREE QUARTERS

When soft September crafts again
her multi-coloured counterpane
and clothes the land in glorious hue
contrasting with the fading blue
of sky where swallows swerve and dip
above hedgerows of haw and hip,
breathe again the breath of rest
and let your soul be gently blessed
by autumn's quiet peacefulness
as summer slips three quarters in the west.

VeeBee

GOLDEN MEMORIES

Golden memories
of hop picking in
Herefordshire,
a bygone age.

Sitting on a tall
three legged stool
in my granny made
red check frock.

Pulling a bind
with my sister.
Collapsing in giggles
as we end in a
heap on the floor.

Eating thick cheese
sandwiches
with black hop
stained hands.

The sound of
"Clear um up!"
"Clear um up!"
as the busheller arrives.

Homeward bound,
enveloped in that
evocative smell,
creating a lifetime
of memories!

Margaret Dallow

INSPIRATION or COLD COMFORT

My beautiful trees
Are getting down
To the bare bones now
Settling down for winter
Letting go all inessentials
Before their journey
Into cold and darkness.

The Ash is ready now
Connected, as it is,
To all three worlds
There will be no wind
Can turn the tide
Of frost and rime.

The Yew tree
Bears a berry
As red as it's
Heartwood.
Albeit the Hornbeam dallies
Delighting in
His coat of many colours.
The Holly smiles
And dresses up
To welcome the Mabon Child
The child of light.

Silver Firs
Smell of tangerines
Redolent of
Christmas stockings
And children's dreams
On Christmas Eve.

Gorse, Mahonia
Hold the dream
Of Beltane's fire
And the turning of the year.

And me, too,
I feel stripped down
To bare essentials.
What do I really know?
Who would mourn my passing?

Where do my achievements stand?
Upon foundations of
Loose and shifting sand.

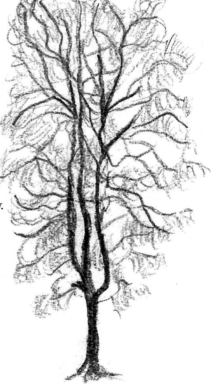

At least I know
When I am gone
The trees I've planted
Will live on
And hold the dream
Of the earth
And the dream of the stars

A dream
They shared with me
But briefly, dimly, fleetingly.

Lawrence Randle

November 2005

WAR AND DEATH

FIGURES ON THE FORESHORE

There are figures on the foreshore of this secluded bay,
Where Preseli river meets the sea,
Meandering unhurriedly, oft pausing in their way,
Arrested by such tranquillity;

Now stooping to inspect some strange creature of the shore,
Or to brush the sand from bright half buried shells.
The witness for their passing will not for long endure,
Erased by the tide the pale moon swells.

When they have gone, returning to unquiet hurried lives,
They leave no tell tale footprints behind –
Yet something intangible of themselves here survives,
Something of their hearts remains enshrined.

Enshrined amongst the loveliness of this lonely place,
Where the scars of man's endeavours are few,
Where insistent wordless whispers proclaim 'glory and grace'
And all with wonder glistens like the dew.

So few will leave a trace on earth of their existence here,
of benefice, or notoriety:
The tide of time obliterates, we mostly disappear;
Sparse words upon a stone our history.

Is life then meaningless as some hasten to say?
Leave we no lasting patterns in the sands?
The risen one of Calvary knows no such dismay –
Nor his followers, their names writ on his hands.

Peter D Hollingsworth

John Ruskin writes of "a continual perception of Sanctity in the whole of nature, from the slightest thing to the vastest, an instinctive awe, mixed with delight, an indefinable thrill... I could only feel this perfectly when alone: and then "it would often make me shiver... with the joy and fear of it"... perhaps something of this "shivering" seeded this poem.

AND THE POPPIES WILL BE FOR EVER RED

Gone are the sword, lance and long bow;
Muskets and chain mail sit in museums now.
The stroke of a politician's pen
Can still fly young men
To fight, live and die
Neath clouds of a foreign sky
Be it a bullet or an arrow
The margins of life are so narrow.
The end can be clean or death can be obscene
For those who won't see the morrow.

The mud and the trenches
The gas and the stenches
Are the horrors we talk about
But we know so little of the hell
And the survivors won't tell
Lest the glories fade of the victories we won
Have we not learnt?
Though in our memory it's burnt
That with all the conflict we've done
Cannot the memory of the bomb
That burnt the heart of the rising sun
Be a warning of wars to come?

Now in the month of November
On the eleventh day we remember
The church clock will declare
That the eleventh hour is here
And all over our land will fall silence in prayer.
Our dead are still dead
And the poppies will be forever red.

Denis R H Teal

CERTAINTY

I had more certainty when I was young
Than I have now my song is three parts sung.
I'm not so clear that certainty is sure
To give us safety – rather it's a lure
T'wards enmity and envy. Each believes
That his own creed is true; a lie deceives
His fellow, who he knows is wrong –
Not just a counterpoint in the great song
That is creation, and the lives we lead,
All huddled on the same Earth where we need;
Co-operation so we may survive;
To work together so we all can thrive,
Unless we can accept that truth has many threads,
We'll spend forever, each one, claiming tails are heads.

We humans, ant-like in a universe
That's huge and old and seemingly perverse,
Seeks certainty like moths a distant flame,
Or we a pocket in a snooker game.
If we could know it all, then we were God,
And that we cannot be though with our mod-
ern science we believe that we are near
To knowing all. But should we not be fear-
ful of attaining such a longed-for state
(But human beings never like to wait!)
If we should reach that goal, there is no need
For faith – there's nowhere left for it to lead –
And mystery's no more, for all's an open book;
We've found out ev'ry thing – there's nowhere else to look.

The certainty of fact is what we long to have,
But we can't bear to think that at the grave
There is no more existence, we are dust –
No differentiation 'twixt the just
And unjust; and it's cripplingly unfair
If, virtuous, we are no longer there
In any shape or form we can conceive.
No wonder many 'gullibly' believe
That there must surely be some way to prove
The music keeps on playing in the groove;
The needle cannot simply from the vinyl rise;
There must be something there 'beyond the skies'!
How can we square this existential circle when
We cannot face the chance of ought outwith our ken.

So here is our conundrum: we need faith,
But not if it's transparent like some wraith.
We have to make it solid and insist
That it is firm and palpable, not mist
That e'er evades our grasping, and that veils
Our sight of certainty, like vapour trails
Without the aircraft that has long since passed
From view. We dare not think creation vast
And we so puny that we do not count;
That God exists we make of no account,
But find we pray when things could not go worse,
As if he were our loving nurs'ry nurse.
If we believe he's there, we fill in the empty gaps
As a cartographer might strive to make his maps.

We value certainty above all else;
We'd like life like the Book of Kells;
Compact and colourful, and black and white;
It tells us what is wrong and what is right.
This means that any other view of life
Inevitably leads to human strife.
We bolster our belief by praying aid
Of God's authority, but it's man made –
Or man transmitted – and we tend to see
What backs the line of our own thinking, be
It ever so contorted or mistook,
Or just because it's 'written in the book'
If only we could all be humble and concede
The chance of error, there is much could be agreed.

Doubt seems uncertain, therefore we would shun
It, but within the cosmos it's the one
Thing that is certain and we all do share;
Like death in life, the fact that must be there.
Doubt is the core of our humanity;
This 'contradiction', often hard to see,
Is what sustains our hope, and means we can
Have much in common with our fellow man.
The road to hell is paved with certainty,
And brings despite, whoever we may be.
God understands that we cannot be sure;
However hard we look, there is no cure.
Man's not unmanned by doubt – it is his staple food –
He knows when tree surrounded that he's in a wood.

John Pare

THE DEEPEST SILENCE

Of all the silences
It seems
Silence of loss
Speaks loudest

It wakes the deepest sleeper
That non-movement
Of a body no longer there.

That non-sounding of a rousing bell
That gives to life a meaning.

The heart-breaking of what can never be.

Celia Rees

ABANDONMENT

In nineteen eighty-two, our nation was at war
With Argentina, o'er the Falkland Isles
A task force expedition had left England's shore
A voyage of eight thousand miles
To face dangers and hardships and trials

Now four hundred Paras were advancing on Goose Green
And the Argentine barracks in the town
It was the fiercest fighting most of us had seen
Then our Colonel – a soldier of renown
The valiant 'H' Jones' was taken down

Two days of ceaseless fighting; ammunition low
We were weary, and hungry, and cold
Our casualties were mounting, and this latest blow
Upon our spirits and our courage told
We knew not what outcome would unfold

I was with Chris Keeble when he assumed command
Upon his face perplexity engraved
The course of this engagement, not as had been planned
Promised little of the victory we craved
Of how our lives and honour might be saved

No military solution could Major Keeble find
But he carried about with him an old prayer
And seeking to quieten his mind
Gave voice to the words printed there
Abandoning his future
To God's care

Then, upon the instruments and weapons of war,
Our leader understood what he must do
And all the apprehension he'd felt before
Was displaced as his conviction grew
And inward peace and confidence he knew

In the morning briefing his proposal was aired:
Surrender terms to offer to our foes –
That from further bloodshed we might all be spared.
Then off to the Argentines he goes;
A white flag of truce above him blows.

Meeting his counterparts and talking face to face
Terms were agreed without delay:
Fifteen hundred soldiers at the Goose Green base –
Conscripted men with small heart for the fray –
Surrendered to the Paras that day.

A dignified surrender – their national anthem sung,
A parade, and the laying down of arms:
But Argentine military lethally stung,
The repressive ruling junta alarmed,
Their ambitions irrevocably harmed.

Goose Green marked the turning point for Major Keeble too,
Though a glittering career seemed assured:
As the 'Prayer of Abandonment' inspires him anew.
He campaigns for a nobler reward:
To broker peace and help promote accord.

Peter D Hollingsworth

"This is a true story, well documented "on line". It is published with the full
consent of Chris Keeble."

WOMEN AT WAR

Men flock to sign, while ladies fear and cheer
Marching hundreds on the path to glory
Doing their bit for all that love holds dear
Most willing, some herded, that's the story.

But what of industry of commerce, life?
For life goes on. There's children to be fed,
Weapons and food to be sent to the strife
Who will do the work and by whom be led?

The roles of girls and women are clear cut
At home with children, housework, hens and ducks
As salesgirls, till they marry, okay. But
Who ever heard of women driving trucks!

Digging and ploughing, herding cows through mud,
Assembling weapons on the factory floor,
Nursing the broken, wading through their blood
No! No lass, that's no way to win a war.

Yet slow and silent, women start to move
Without complaint, a long and constant drive,
Unstoppable intention, set to prove
That in their hands their country still will thrive.

So men will have, the food, clothes, guns to fight.
There's nothing they won't do, and wide their scope
To keep the home fires burning with a light
In which to build a future, love, growth, hope.

Celia Rees

THE GUNNER'S HORSE

He stroked to quiet the horse's quivering flanks,
Talking while he brushed the turgid clay
That clung and spattered once white feathers.

Beneath the bellow of guns he whispered,
His voice breaking he breathed assurances
Calming his own terrors to keep control.

He kept on talking his horse responding,
Harness quickly slid in place, reins gathered
Together man and beast acted as one.

Slowly sucked from a morass of mud
The cocking horse pulled the chaise of death
Out of Flanders' mire.

Slackened reins, knees gripped the horse's side,
The carriage gathered pace, sliding and slipping
Towards the new Front Line.

Barbara M Stewart

HUMOUR

THE CABBAGE

There is a cabbage in our garden
So big and fat and round
He sits there like a king
In that red fertile ground.

He had his photo taken
Measured every day
He's really been quite pampered
In a cabbage sort of way.

Would we ever eat him?
I rather think not.
They say they are known to shriek
When pulled from the plot.

So we look upon him as a friend
That cabbage in our garden
So big and fat
And round.

Margaret Dallow

This poem is dedicated to a little girl called Harriet who learnt this
poem from her grandma's toilet wall and stood up when she went
to school and recited it off by heart.

PRAISE POEM TO THE WORM

You are:
an earth excavator soil swallower
dark-time wanderer leaf mould lover
farmland genius and garden expert.

You are:
a peristaltic pedestrian on footless feet
ring bearing ready saddled
sightless navigator and night seer.

You are:
a miniscule mouth moving megaliths
a leaf analyst casting loam
dedicated expert and eminent engineer

You are:
a continent crossing barrier smashing
globe gallivanting bird shunning
compost creating universal leveller.

"Wonderful" said Worm.

Gill Fothergill

FOOL'S GOLD

It was a damp grey morning of April the first, meandering along at around five miles a fortnight along the lazy winding lanes from Avenbury. The dogs having had the highlight of their day were settled in the back thinking of their butcher's tripe and bonio, and me thinking of black pudding, white pudding, tomatoes, crispy fat bacon and fatty fried bread (my Daughter says "That's the sort of food that makes folk dead.") Hah! Out of the corner of my eye, in the hedgerow a horned Ram I did espy, not that unusual I hear you say, but when you are told this horned Ram had horns of shiny gold!! No, forget it, put it out of your mind! I must be getting old! How absurd! A Ram with horns of "shiny gold."

Now later in the day, shopping for the lethal ingredients for my morrow's breakfast, the conversation with Mervyn, who has a flock in Avenbury lane turned to sheep. I casually said, "I saw a roaming Ram, to identify was not hard." And Mervyn said, "Yes, I found him munching hay inside my yard. I put him in my barn and when I shut the door he went absolutely berserk as though he had never been shut in before." I tentatively asked, "Was there anything unusual about this feral sheep?" "Hah," said Merv, after a pause, "he had probably escaped from Little Bo Peep, his one eye was blue the other black, and his horns were shiny and gold." I said "Thank heaven for that." With all marbles accounted for, the tale can now be told.

Said Mervyn, "I rang the police to say a wandering Ram I had found. I caught him eating hay inside my barn compound." In a Dixon of Dock Green voice, the constable asked had this errant animal got any identifying marks upon his back? "No," said Merv, but his one eye is blue and the other is black." Then added, "Oh! And his horns are shiny gold." After a lengthy pause, the Dixon tone changed to a Ken Dodd attitude, he said, "Well Sir, having taken a look down the columns of my lost property book, we have a flock of sheep in our lost dog pen, and their fleeces are of spun gold. Bring yours in, Jason has been told."

Denis R H Teal

JUST A POTATO

Roast potato
I'm the brown skinned one
All crusty and ready for the meat
I never look all neat.

Chips
Oh I'm all divided up
And turned into heaps of gold
Ready for a finger hold.

Crisps
I've been put in a pack
I come with a bunch
And a rattley crunch.

Jacket potato
I'm the big male potato
Who wears the jacket
I can hack it!

New potato
I'm the little new potato
Small and delicate
Growing up I can't wait!

Mashed potato
Oh what have they done to me?
I was round and chubby
Now I'm soft and blubby!

Judy Malet

SALAD SONATA

Iceberg is a cool dude
He fancies red pepper so lush
But tasty tomato is giving him the eye
Edging nearer, almost to touch.

Cool cucumber is on the scene
And celery's stalking around
Red onion decides to back out of the game
To the grapes he is honour bound.

Mayonnaise drapes herself leisurely over
The salad, the ham and the chips
And vinegar is left out this time
As he stands to attention and drips.

Salty cellar has been shaken again
It is all too much to bear
Demolish, demolish, swim with the wine
Puds are following up from the rear.

And cheese and biscuits
And coffee white
And a choc, mint
Good-night!

Shirley Whittall

MEGHALAYA CLOUD TEA

India's gods are thirsty and desire cloud tea!
Their servants sing, "Vishnu, we require cloud tea!"

Did Mahavira, Durga and Medha
And all the gods of India inspire cloud tea?

Her neighbours are Darjeeling and Assam;
Megahala, where the gods acquire cloud tea!

The Gilded Teapot praises this estate's sweet leaves
"If Lakschmi were to sweat she would perspire cloud tea!"

Gold starred, brass rolled and full of shiny tip
Wake us up from worry and from Maya, cloud tea!

In dhoti, painted bindi or kameez
All those who sip this second flush suspire, "Cloud tea!"

Go, brew some nectar from these wild green forest hills
And with Tea Poet, Darcy Jones – admire cloud tea!

Elizabeth Darcy Jones

'suspire' = sigh

I AM AN AMOEBA

I am a small amoeba, and live inside a pond,
I'm in what's been referred to as, the slough of despond,
and since I live down in the mud; this seems to correspond.

I'm a little like a blood cell, that's called a phagocyte,
[that's not a heavy smoker, in case you think it might!]
engulfing food, what ere I get, by day and in the night.

Ok, so I'm just a single cell,
but I spend time just thinking things like; 'what the hell',
since I know several people with brains like that as well!

You see, I'm only a small bit of basic protoplasm,
a shapeless, shifting, changing lump; a quite amorphous spasm,
and my brain would never qualify, it's just a tiny chasm,

My stomach is a vacuole, I've neither mouth nor gob,
and intellectually I'm quite a silly sod,
like Steve McQueen some years ago, I'm really just a blob.

I haven't any armpits, since I don't have any arms,
I keep myself close to me, and out of the way of harms,
among my many talents, I have neither qualms nor charms.

I don't wear any knickers and never need a bra,
No legs to ride a bike with; I could never drive a car,
And I will never be seen at, nor get called to, the bar.

And since I was born leg-less, I'm seldom worse for drink,
I don't have ears to hear with, I can't hear plunk or plink,
I don't have eyes to weep with, and I cannot even blink,

No nose, so I can't dribble, and I don't feel this a shame,
can't poke where it's not wanted, and gets therefore no blame,
can't tell my arse from elbow, they're both one and the same.

I seldom ever feel like sex, I've nothing real to give,
to tell the truth I haven't much to really have sex with,
or else, though rather stupidly, in two I split, forthwith.

So there, I'm an Amoeba and perhaps enigma too,
though not one of Elgar's, no Nimrod me, that's true,
and you will never find me in anybody's zoo.

I'd love to have some features and arms and legs and things,
to be more like a person and go and play on swings,
and give to all the charities, and flag days in the spring.

Yes, if I was human, with hands and trouser pocket,
I'm sure I would be generous, give freely and not mock it,
but you can't be philanthropic, when you're only microscopic.

Dave Hubble

ON HEARING SOMETHING ON RADIO 4
ABOUT PLASTIC DAFFODILS AT GRASMERE!

Wordsworth, thou shouldst be living at this hour to see a host beside
yon sparkling lake
A silent host of plastic, for God's sake,
Monstrosities pretending to be flowers –
See how th'appalled tourist has to cower
And wonders if he's dreaming or awake
While Chinese factory workers help to make
A right old profit. Well, don't be so sour;
Yon crags, computer generated to enthral,
Yon lake, a hologram to sparkle more,
Yon sheep, whose bleat's a synthesizer's call,
Yon boat, projected on the farther shore –
I think I'll lie upon my flabby belly
And vacant still and pensive, switch on the telly.

Thalia Gordon Clark

THE NATURAL WORLD

SEASPELL

Come down to the beach with me
Come right down with me to the sea.
We can look for pebbles all for free.

We might find a scribble stone
They talk a lot, a fact well known.

Moon stones have a quieter sound
Goddess stones are the ones with a hole.

No two stones are ever the same
Each has its song, its story and a name.

Look how the pebbles shine in the sun
When blessed by the sea, every one.

They tell of earthquakes, volcanoes and forgotten skies.
Look a red beetle and a butterfly.

There's a beautiful shell, adrift on the sand
There is a snake stick, they make very good wands.

Just when you think you've found one stone's twin
The sea gives a tug and hauls it in,

Or you turn it over and it's not quite right.
You look away and it's out of sight.

You've found a pretty cake stone
And it's reminded you of tea.

It's good on the beach, just you and me.

Lawrence Randle

I wrote this for Finlay, Isabel's older brother. At the time he
was full of insatiable curiosity, and obsessed with cake.

CREATION

The fresh green leaves adorn the trees,
All vibrant greens of different shade;
The bursting buds and blossom fine
All seem so much designed to please;
But I am told they are not made
Nor I, so where to draw the line?

A magpie flies up from the ground,
A flash of black and white in air;
A pigeon clatters from the boughs
Through foliage thick spread all around;
But why do I perceive them fair,
If chance alone their life allows?

The sunlight glistens on the grass
Bedewed this early in the morn;
The colours sparkle on my eyes;
But why should all this come to pass,
If it is chance, I am forlorn;
If I am too,
I am not wise.

The moonshine casts a gentle light;
It throws soft shadows, unlike the sun
That shines more harshly, though with heat
Enabling life in all its height
And breadth and depth its course to run;
If not designed, it's very neat.

John Pare

WAS IT?

Walking the dogs
Working out the day's events
An inner prompting came, to listen.
Was it?
Did I?
Yes. I did.
Cuckoo, cuckoo,
In the distance,
Almost muffled.

I continue to listen.
Nothing! Was it?
Did I?

Ah! There again,
Still far off
But further south
Cuckoo, cuckoo
And again
Cuckoo, cuckoo,
And further west
Cuckoo, cuckoo.

Oh Wonder Bird,
Our harbinger of spring,
Usually here by mid April

Late this year, a week
Through into May.
Cuckoo, cuckoo.

So well known to Shakespeare
And many other poets...
Cuckoo, cuckoo.
So well recognised, but who can
Recognise by sight and
Not by sound...Cuckoo.

This bird of such pernicious habit,
So uncaring of reed warbler, dunnock and pipit.
Have you heard the cuckoo?
Notorious emblem used by Beethoven, Delius and Handel.
Cuckoo...cuckoo.

Cuckoo. So well known,
So mysterious,
Fantastic science has enabled
Sleuth RSPB
To trace five birds from Norfolk,
Across Europe, by different routes
And on to Equatorial Africa.
Five set out and five started to return.
Only two arrived sadly! Forty per cent!

People of England, Wake Up.
The cuckoo, that integral part of the English scene
And many more beside are disappearing.
Do you care?

CUCKOO   Cuckoo   cuck   oooo.........

Bryony Cullum

May 10th. 2012

CAN YOU HEAR THE BUTTERFLY
SOFT AS THISTLEDOWN?

JD

SONG OF THE EARTH

Can you hear the grass growing?
Can you smell the pines?
Can you hear the earth
Drinking up the rain?
Can you hear the sound of silence
As snow falls to the ground?
Can you hear the trees cry
as the woodman cuts them down?
Can you hear the whisper of the corn
And the sound of insects rustling under ground?
Can you hear the bees busy making honey
and the humming birds humming?
Can you hear the butterfly,
Soft as thistledown?
Can you hear the hush
Before the thunderstorm?
Can you hear? Can you hear
The song of the earth?

Jane Dallow

AFTER FELLING

Here was something terrible
in how they lay,
full stretch,
Each shared its weight,
Bark peeling,
Offering sweet odour
to the rain rinsed air.

Majestic.
A hundred feet of years
Branches, now a memory
told in exquisite scar.
And each great trunk felled
Reveals the secret ballot
Of its age.

Thalia Gordon Clark

THE VALLEY THROUGH THE WINDOW

Through the window gazing at the valley below
Into the morning's light I watch.
The sun rises slowly beyond the distant hills.
I see the misty silver thread that winds along the river bed.
The sun, its rays, and cloudy shadows
Drift across the hills and meadows.
Golden beams alight upon the dew.
They warm the new ploughed earth;
Secrets sown beneath will be the promise made for spring.
I turn and see the willows swaying in the breeze
And in a magic moment become a silver sea.
The lime leaves once a vivid green are yellowing
And float gently down to lie among the grass.
Great and ancient copper beech with branches spread so wide;
Its leaves are changing too.
I see into the distance and set against the sky
Tall straight poplars planted long ago
Landmarks for travellers passing to and fro.
The valley's ever changing seasons bring each its joy,
The brightest greens of spring
Summer's golden touch and autumn's darker hues.
Winter wind and rain so cold
And when the valley's white with snow
A winter's scene of wonderment it brings;

Its past pleasures echo through my mind.
To know the only changes made
Are those of nature's own.

Josie Ann Dolan

This was Ann's first major poem. It tells of the view she had from her room
at the cottage at Avenbury where she was born; a place very dear to her.

THE MIRACLE OF THE GARDEN

The garden is dull-brown and grey,
Bundles of dry twigs cling to trellises.
Trees are lifeless, the summer house is cold and dusty,
Dead leaves piled up in every nook and cranny.
Flower pots are choked with frost-dead geraniums.
March; one weekend of sunshine –
Sweeping, chopping, pruning, dusting, visiting the tip.
The clocks go forward and suddenly winter is gone.
Sun shining, tulips glowing,
Blossom flowering, wood pigeons calling
(Grass needs cutting)
Pansies smiling from the flower pots,
The summer house welcomes us in.
The miracle of the garden is happening again.

Dorothy Kennedy

WHISTLE DOWN THE WIND

Trees swaying, sighing, bowing, bending;
Leaves scattering, rustling, bustling
Like hustlers hustling,
Swirling, turning, lifting in the wind.

Children squealing, screaming, dancing, singing;
Mothers shouting, hurrying, scurrying,
Never doubting the madness of the wind.

March hares on hind legs, boxing,
Eyes bulging with excitement
As the sap starts rising.
Mad March hares everywhere
Running like the wind.

And the blackbird sits hidden
In the old oak tree…
Whistling down the wind.

Jane Dallow

A COLOURFUL DAY

Soft colours revealed by dawn,
Grey, yellow, pink dissipated into
Blue sky, intentless, with white fluffy clouds,
Bright sunlight, highly defining.

Travelling through North Herefordshire we see
Countryside, lush, green with many hues,
Splashed banks of pink campion companion to delicate frothy Queen Ann's lace
Overlook buttercup yellow fields.

Brushing the Welsh, Shropshire border
Steep hills stretch to the sky,
Covered with dark conifer stands, relieved by lighter deciduous trees
Enclosing fields of ghostly, freshly shorn sheep
Or in flatter glaciated valleys, cattle rich brown, cream, black or pied.

Llanfairwaterdine, a gem amongst the hills,
Valley sides streaked with bluebell haze,
A corner dazzles us with orange and yellow Welsh Poppies,
A picturesque pub with stall of plants
And pots including mulberry jam!

Our kaleidoscope was unfinished.
A statuesque giant angelica at Horse and Groom,
Offa's Dyke country showing off profusions of white May,
Finally, relaxing in Bleddfa's hospitality,
Bemused by artists' colourations.

A British summer day clarifying landscape at its best,
Each moment to be taken and enjoyed

Stored for future recollection
"I will lift mine eyes unto the hills from whence cometh my help."

Bryony Cullum

June 5th. 2010

This poem was written after an amazing, beautiful day out with a friend who
was looking for a place to live in the area.

ROSEMARIE'S VISION

Sitting in my doorway,
Letting the peace of the countryside seep into me
I have a sudden soft intake of breath;
Just down below me, a brown hare!

He pauses,
Eyes, ears, alert, nose twitching,
He sits and pays attention to his paws,
Then to those amazing ears
And those long, powerful, elegant hind feet.

He settles down
Absorbing warmth from the gravel,
Relaxing, his ears fold.
Unknown to this brown hare,
He and I share moments of tranquillity.

Bryony Cullum

(As told to me by Rosemarie over the phone)

THE PEREGRINE FALCON

Gliding high over the peaks of the old Shropshire hills
On a hot summer's day, or over winter's snow clad crests
Past heather covered slopes, clearest tumbling streams
Searching for some hapless prey far beneath, is his quest

For woe betide the labouring wild fowl flying far beneath
The Grouse showing briefly above the old bracken's rust
A Raptor, with agility, speed unmatched drops in his stoop
Then puffballs of aimless feathers float down into the dust

Living quite successfully in most countries of the world
This truly magnificent falcon, the Emperor of the skies
Acquired through centuries by noblemen of high birth
Renowned, revered and respected, to own it a huge prize

His world the rocky headlands and rugged sea salted cliffs
Of the high remote moorland, or mountainous craggy peaks
Arid deserts of the world pass beneath his bowed wings
Piercing eyes seeing all from his dark moustached cheeks

One morning I heard him call high in the Salopian hills
His Hak Hak Hak echoing down midst the rocks and scree
Just a speck in the sky, searching for some prey far below
Oh would that he forever flies wild and flies free.

John Elmes   *Tiercel of the March*

And finally…

THE LONG AND SHORT OF IT!

Some say my poems are too long,
(I think some are too short),
But please my readers, I must try;
Yes this I really ought.
So right or wrong; I say in short,
I'm going now; so long!

Dave Hubble

Read by Dave's request at his funeral.

Index of poets

Bryony Cullum *33, 92, 100, 101*

Jane Dallow *21, 95, 98*

Margaret Dallow *60, 63, 80*

Sophia Dimmock *17, 52, 54*

Josie Ann Dolan *14, 37, 97*

John Elmes – Tiercel of the March *51, 56, 102*

Gill Fothergill *81*

Charles Gordon Clark *32, 48, 55*

Thalia Gordon Clark *43, 88, 96*

Peter Holliday *18, 53, 61*

Peter D Hollingsworth *68, 73*

Dave Hubble *28, 47, 86, 105*

Elizabeth Darcy Jones *19, 42, 85*

Dorothy Kennedy *29, 36, 98*

Judy Malet *42, 54, 83*

Maggie McGladdery *40, 44, 49*

John Pare *35, 70, 91*

Lawrence Randle *10, 41, 64, 90*

Val Randle *16, 46*

Celia Rees *25, 73, 76*

Barbara M Stewart *24, 62, 77*

Denis R H Teal *14, 69, 82*

VeeBee (Valerie Ball) *22, 30, 62*

Shirley Whittall *50, 84*